BLACKJACK TO WIN

A Layman's Guide to Beating the Game

The Grey Knight

Table of Contents

Acknowledgements

The author wishes to acknowledge the contribution of Mr. Sandy K., who began me on my blackjack odyssey some years ago. Mr. K. permitted me to avail myself of his extensive blackjack library and computer printouts, and taught me much about casino tactics. He learned these from experience, since he is unfortunately barred from playing in Nevada.

I also wish to thank Mr. Lawrence Revere and Professor Thorp - although I never met these gentlemen, their works contributed much to my success. Finally, I wish to thank my family - my wife for putting up with many evenings of cards and chips spread on the dining room table, and my children for dealing countless hands in the early days.

Preface

The French invented blackjack around the same time they invented the guillotine, their other fun game. This should tell you something. They called blackjack vingt-et-un, which means 21, and the guillotine the guillotine.

The guillotine blade weighs over 100 pounds and works in about 3/4 of a second. The vingt-et-un deck weighs a few ounces and is somewhat slower. The guillotine works once on the player, but vingt-et-un can repeat many times.

If you can readily see the similarities from experience, then this book is for you.

BLACKJACK TO WIN

"Will you walk into my parlor, said a spider to a fly." -
"The Spider and the Fly", Mary Howitt

1 Introduction

Like many classically interesting games, blackjack consists of a few elemental rules, easily learned, within lies the framework for complex and intelligent strategy. Few such games offer the incentive to learn and play well as blackjack.

The player endeavors to come closer to 21 than the dealer, and bets even money that he will. He is dealt two cards, as is the dealer, and has the option of asking for additional cards in an attempt to improve his total. Should he exceed 21, he loses. The dealer must take additional cards until he reaches or exceeds 17. The player is not so constrained. If the dealer exceeds, he "busts", and the player wins. The catch is that the player goes first, and if he busts, he loses regardless of the dealer's subsequent actions. All other rules and strategies are designed to assist in overcoming that built-in edge. This book presents such strategies.

The reader may be aware that there are several blackjack books available. Some contain workable strategies. Then why this one?

It is the author's view that the study methods and guide-lines for implementation presented in the past are in-adequate. In the end, the width of your wallet is the sole measure of success in blackjack - not the extent of mem-orized tables and rules. Study, practice and implement-ation are paramount. I have tried to present the material so that it can be learned efficiently and used in a practical manner.

There is little room for error in successful blackjack play. The casinos know this. Many people come to Las Vegas and try to count cards. Look at the number of blackjack tables in the average casino, as compared to the space allotted to other gaming pastimes, and it will become apparent that success has come only to the very few. Miscount, and all strategy works against you. Play under unfavorable conditions such as weariness or too many other players at the table, and you will probably lose. Make two mistakes an hour even under ideal conditions, and you will have lost your edge.

Still, blackjack can be beaten. During 1980, Atlantic City opened its doors to card counters and was decimated. This experiment, designed to last two weeks, was abruptly terminated early as casino losses ran into the millions. Blackjack is hard work, but you will be pursuing your goal under pleasant conditions, for the most part, and the game can be very rewarding. Crass as it may sound, there are few material things in life as enjoyable as accumulating and spending money you have skillfully won.

Blackjack cannot be beaten unless the player counts cards, and counts them accurately. This is difficult and demands constant practice. If each playing session were a test, you must score 96% or better or lose. There are only two grades - A and F. There are thousands of F's being handed out in Las Vegas every day.

This is not meant to discourage, but rather emphasize the necessity for diligent effort. Blackjack is a serious business and learning most of a system is tantamount to throwing your money away. It can go chillingly fast as it is. You must learn to play as a set of totally conditioned responses - much like reciting your address while riding a bicycle and reading street signs at the same time. As the beer ad says, "Practice, practice, practice."

The player can just about break even without counting, using the basic strategy presented herein. If you decide that counting and learning the entire book is not worth the effort, or that you would make a significant number of errors counting no matter how long you practiced, then by all means learn the basic strategy. You will be relying on luck to win, but will have at least maximized your chances. If, somehow, you are also able to notice when an excess of small cards have been played as opposed to tens and aces, and increase your bet size somewhat in those situations, you may win. Even a perfect count, however, will seldom give you more than about a 4% edge at times. Counting, in part, is designed to notify you when the deck is in your favor so you may increase your bet size accordingly.

Presented in the pages that follow is a plus-minus strategy that does work. More complex systems have been devised which can win at slightly higher rates, but the author feels these are largely unworkable. An inordinate amount of time and mental manipulation is required and the result is error-prone.

The goals of this book are to teach you a moderate understanding of why card counting works, present a system for its use, and provide clear detailed instruction as to how to learn, practice, and implement. I have also attempted to pass along information about the casinos themselves under actual playing conditions which can be of benefit. The rest is up to you.

Let's get to it.

"Give me a fish and I can eat a meal. Teach me to fish and I can eat for a lifetime."   - Unknown

2 Rules of the Game

Blackjack is played with anywhere from one to six decks of cards, from which all jokers have been removed. (There are enough jokers already seated at the table.) All players play against the dealer and not each other. The dealer represents the house; all bets are against his hand. A maximum of seven players may engage in the game at one time, coming and going with each individual hand at will.

In order to play, it is necessary to place a bet in the betting circle or square in front of the player's seat. The bet is placed before the dealer deals any cards for the particular hand.

Before play initially begins, the cards are thoroughly shuffled by the dealer. Shuffling must be accomplished so that the plane of the cards does not violate the plane of the table; they are never lifted from thc flat position. This is to prevent accidental exposure of any card face. When shuffling is completed, a player designated at the whim of the dealer is offered the opportunity to cut the cards. This is usually done with a plastic divider card.

10

If the game uses more than two decks, the divider card is inserted (somewhat arbitrarily) approximately one full deck in front of the rear of the card stack by the dealer. The cards are then placed in a shoe, at the dealer's left. The shoe is a slanted card box designed to permit one card only to be removed from it at a time. It is chained to the table to prevent switching an entire shoe, which has happened at least once.

If the deck or decks (maximum of two) are to be hand-held, the plastic card is placed on the bottom.

In either situation, the next event is the "burn." The top card is not dealt to any player, but rather discarded, except in certain London casinos who may have now discontinued the practice. In a shoe game, the first card is slipped out of the shoe and moved face downward across the table to the discard pile, to the dealer's right. With a hand held deck, the burn card is either dealt with similarly or inverted underneath the plastic card. Now housekeeping is done and play begins.

The dealer deals a card clockwise around the table to each seat which has placed a bet. The bet itself must be no less than the table minimum, and no greater than the table maximum. These amounts, usually from $2 to $1,000 on the Las Vegas strip, are normally indicated by a sign on the corner of the table, or directly above it. Most of these signs are difficult or impossible to read except on the higher stake tables, where they seem to leap out at you.

If the dealer is dealing from one deck, the player cards are always face down. If multiple decks are used, the cards are often face up. After each player has received an initial card, the dealer will deal himself one card face down. After the second card to the player, the dealer receives his second card face up.

At that point the dealer begins to poll each player in turn to determine whether he wishes to draw any additional cards, unless the dealer's up card is an ace or ten value card. A ten value card is an actual ten, king, queen or jack. If the dealer's up card is a ten value card, he must check for blackjack, which is a combination of an ace and a ten value card in the first two cards only. If an ace is underneath, the dealer must turn over his bottom card and collect all the player bets, as blackjack is an unbeatable hand. Should any player also have a blackjack, this is a stand-off, or "push", which nobody wins.

If the dealer's up card is an ace, an additional opportunity for a side bet may be availed. This is called insurance. The dealer will ask all players if they want to insure their initial bet by asking "Insurance?" twice. The players then have the opportunity to bet an amount up to half the amount of their original bets, thus wagering that the dealer does indeed have a blackjack. This bet is placed in the arc in front of the betting circle labelled, logically enough, Insurance.

If the dealer does not have blackjack, he collects all the insurance bets without revealing the identity of his down card and play continues. If he has blackjack, he turns over his ten value card and collects all bets in the betting circles except those for which insurance has been wagered. A winning insurance bet pays two to one, and thus no chips exchange for the hand in question. The player has protected, or insured, his initial bet.

If a player has blackjack and the dealer does not, he customarily turns over his two cards (unless they are already face up) and the dealer pays him 1.5 times his original bet. Note in contrast that a dealer blackjack collects only the amount of the original player bet.

Without a dealer blackjack, then, the dealer begins polling each player in turn clockwise to determine if the player wishes to stand with his two cards as dealt or take one of three possible alternate courses of action: hit, split a pair, or double down. The player, in order to win, must come closer to a total of 21 in his hand than the dealer does. Should a player hit and exceed the allowed

21 total, he immediately loses and his bet is collected along with his cards. The player is allowed to draw as many cards as he wishes in his endeavor to near or reach the 21 total. All cards count their face value with the exception of the ace, which may be one or eleven at the player's discretion. When the player has drawn as many cards as he feels appropriate without busting, the dealer addresses the next player and the action is repeated.

As stated, the player has two other options he may wish to avail himself of. This is doubling down and splitting pairs. Pair splitting means that the player has received two cards of equal rank and desires to play them as separate hands. To split a pair, the player places the two cards side by side, face up, and places an additional wager equal to his initial bet alongside the second card. This indicates to the dealer that the player is playing two hands and he will place another card face up by each of the original pair cards. The player then has the option of hitting or standing on each hand, but the hands are played sequentially. He must finish one hand before addressing the other.

Usually after a pair is split the player cannot double down on either hand. He may, however, split his cards again if another card of the same rank is mated with one of the split cards. In this manner it is possible to wager a total amount up to four times the table limit.

Should the player split aces, he is permitted one additional card only on each ace, dealt face down. If he receives a ten value card, the hand is treated as 21 and not blackjack.

Doubling down means that the player wishes one additional card only, which is placed face down in a single deck game. To do this he must place an amount equal to his initial bet alongside the first amount. The player is betting he can come closer to 21 than the dealer by drawing only one additional card.

Some casinos restrict the combinations of cards which are eligible for doubling down. This always works against the player. Examples would be when doubling is permitted on totals of 9, 10, or 11 only, or just 10 or 11.

When all players have completed their actions, the dealer will turn up his down card. The dealer must hit until he reaches a minimum of 17. When this total is reached, or anything greater, he must stop. While the player may value the ace as either one or eleven, usually the dealer has no choice when computing whether he must hit or not. For instance, an ace and a six is seventeen to the dealer and he must stand. If the dealer has an ace and a five, and when hitting receives a seven, for instance, the ace is now regarded as one and the dealer has not busted.

In many casinos the dealer must hit a "soft" 17, which is the ace and six. While many players think this is an advantage for them, it is not.

If the dealer busts, he pays off all players one to one except those who have previously busted. Previous bets on bust hands have been collected. If the dealer has not busted, his total is compared to each player's total in turn and the winner is determined by who has the higher total without exceeding 21. A tie is a null, and the player bet is left alone.

The games continue until the deck or decks require reshuffling. If more than two decks are being used, the location of the plastic divider card determines the reshuffle point. The card usually appears in the middle of a hand; in that case play continues uninterrupted and the decks reshuffled at the conclusion of the hand.

In a hand-held game (one or two decks), the cards are reshuffled at the dealer's discretion. Originally, reshuffling occurred when too few cards would remain to deal another complete hand, based upon the number of players at the table. Therefore a one on one game would result in the cards being dealt almost to the end, which is no longer the case today.

The player signals his intended actions with his hand, not his mouth. The player is not supposed to hold his cards with two hands, touch his bet after it has been made, or go behind the table.

A minority of casinos play with certain rule variations. The most common is known as surrender, and allows the player a fifth option. If he feels he will lose after surveying his initial hand and the dealer's up card, the player may surrender his hand at that point and lose half his original bet. This option may be used as part of a winning strategy.

There are still a few gaming establishments which will pay an extra sum when the player receives a total of five or six cards without going over. This is designed to encourage the player to bust and is a successful casino tactic.

There are also casinos who deal both dealer cards face up. In adequate compensation for this, all ties go to the dealer.

Those are the rules. When any unusual or untoward situation arises, the pit boss has the function of arbitrating disputes.

3 Blackjack Theory

The essence of blackjack theory is designed to achieve two essential goals, both of which must be accomplished in order to win money:

1. Notify the player when the deck is favorable to him, so that he will bet more at those times than he would otherwise.

2. Direct the player to hit, stand, double down, split pairs, take insurance or surrender in such a manner as to maximize his chances of winning based upon his cards, the current status of the remaining deck, *and* the likelihood of the dealer busting as indicated by his up card.

Let's take these one at a time.

Blackjack is a game of chance whereby past occurrences influence future events. A finite number of cards with a known composition begins play and random cards - unless somebody is cheating - are removed as the game progresses. Obviously, if we are playing single deck blackjack and four aces appear in the first two hands, no blackjacks will appear until the deck is reshuffled. (They don't seem to appear very often anyway, at least from the player's side of the table.) Other more subtle mathematical conclusions are true. This is not the case with roulette or craps, for example, where independent statistical trials occur.

An awareness of what cards have been dealt, and thus what cards remain, is gained by card counting. This enables the player to judge if the remaining deck is "good" or "bad." The more comprehensive the card counting system, the better picture is gleaned by the player.

A good deck contains an excess of tens and aces over small cards, and a bad deck has the converse. Why is this so? Does not the deck favor or disfavor the dealer and player equally?

The answer is no, for several reasons. The dealer must hit his hand at 16 and below. The player can make an intelligent decision whether to hit or not based upon the situation. Remember also the player acts first and if he busts, the hand is over.

An excess of large cards remaining increases the dealer's likelihood of busting. If this is known prior to the deal, the player must increase his bet size for the particular hand about to be dealt. Thus, he will be betting more heavily when odds are best for him, and that is the key to point one above.

Additionally, blackjacks are more likely to occur when the remaining cards are ten and ace rich. While this is equally true for the dealer, blackjack pays the player 1.5 to 1; a dealer blackjack collects only the original player bet.

Note that the player receives one of his cards before the dealer, and the count may shift before the dealer receives his card. When there are other players at the table, a count advantage may become diluted or lost before the player receives his hand.

Now let us examine point two, which is more subtle.

You will learn and memorize a set of tables which dictates what action will be taken under all conceivable situations, based upon three conditions:

1. Your two up cards as dealt.
2. The dealer's up card.
3. The status of the remaining deck at the time.

It can readily be seen that the player's actions should be influenced by the status of the remaining cards. To illustrate, assume a player total of 14 and a favorable deck. The player would be hesitant to draw realizing an excess of tens remain. Likewise, a player would be encouraged to draw if he knew an excess of small cards remain, as the likelihood of improving his hand without busting is enhanced.

However, it must be realized that the dealer's up card strongly tempers what action must be taken by the player. In our example, if the dealer shows a five there is no conceivable realistic situation which would dictate a player hit, with a 14 total. He must stand, and allow the dealer to suffer the probability of going over.

Let's run through this 14 vs. 5 hand. Assume we are not counting and the player holds his 14 as an 8-6. Considering his hand alone, the decision to hit would be straightforward.

In single deck blackjack, he can draw any of the 50 remaining cards. Of these, any of the following improves his hand:

> the four aces
>
> the four twos
>
> the four threes
>
> the four fours
>
> the four fives
>
> the remaining three sixes
>
> the four sevens
> _____
>
> 27 total cards

The following cards will bust the hand:

> the remaining three eights
> the four nines
> the sixteen ten value cards (10, J, Q, K)
> _____
> 23 total cards

Based solely on the above, a hit is in order. But we must take into account the dealer. The first step is to remove from the above calculation the up card he shows, which is the five. Now of the 49 possible cards for the player to draw, 26 are favorable and 23 are not. Still a hit situation.

What about the dealer's five? We don't know his down card but we can calculate the bust odds for each possible combination of down card and the five. The dealer must hit because his maximum two card total is 16. If, for example, his down card is a ten value the odds are he will bust, as of the remaining 48 cards 22 will improve his hand and 26 will exceed 21. If the down card is a nine, he can draw 26 improving cards and 22 bust cards. And so on.

This is not the end of the calculation, though. Suppose the dealer draws an ace or a two. He must hit again with a down card of nine. The next calculation would be the odds of drawing an improving card vs. a bust card from the remaining 47 cards. The dealer's chances are now considerably poorer, especially with the two. Another small card has been removed from the remaining deck.

From here on it begins to get complex, when we begin factoring in multiple hits for both sides, and the player's various options: pair splitting and doubling down. Eventually we arrive at the player's mathematical preferential choice of action, which maximizes his chances of achieving a higher total than the dealer, while taking into account the chances of each busting. It is vital that the analysis allow for the rule that the player draws first, since if he busts the hand is over. Ties are not relevant since they are stand-offs.

19

It can be seen that the greater the number of other players at the table, the greater random chance will influence the player's outcome. Even if the card counting player is able to see each player card, as is the case with a multiple deck up game, he will only be able to adjust his playing strategy when his turn comes but his bet is already down. A large bet under favorable count conditions may be inappropriate as a result of this. The ideal game is one on one with the dealer.

By counting cards we improve our knowledge of the universe of possibilities and in turn are able to improve the quality of our decision table. The decision table calculations when considering the count become vastly more complex than a non-count matrix, as we must allow for the large number of remaining deck situations. The table tells us the best action to take for every possible situation. With no counting situation, we approximate for general conditions. The better our method of counting, the more accurate will be our decision table.

The rationale shown above is an attempt to portray the relationships between the three factors which govern the player's actions at all times. It is a light brush, to be sure. It is not vital for you to prove or comprehend completely all the mathematical logic which defines and dictates each strategic move, but a conceptual understanding is very helpful when a lot of money is on the line and you grit your teeth and hit a 16, for example, against the dealer's seven.

Remember, it is the combination of all three factors which determines your response and that is why the decision tables are organized in that manner.

Historically, the first scientific inroads were made only about twenty years ago towards beating the game of blackjack. This was the work of Edward O. Thorp, Ph. D., Professor of Mathematics at the University of California at Irvine. Professor Thorp realized the nature of the relationships we have touched on above, and devised a successful simple basic strategy. As he continued to develop his theories, he progressed through a ten count strategy and finally point count systems of ever-increasing complexity. So successful was Professor Thorp that he alone was responsible for major rule changes in the Nevada casinos, designed to nullify his advantage.

These rule changes were short-lived. The game lost its appeal and the original rules had to be reinstated. The casinos began to rely on observing betting sequences of suspected card counters. The customary pattern was a series of small bets culminating in excessively large wagers towards the end of the deck, when the deck was ten-rich. In response, the casinos began reshuffling the cards early. More on this in a later chapter.

Professor Thorp's systems still work today, with the exception that his original betting schemes cannot be used as the casinos have caught on. His *Beat the Dealer* can purchased in its updated edition. It is recommended as background reading.

After Professor Thorp pioneered the way, others added refinements and improvements to the strategies. Julian Braun of IBM in particular contributed in this regard. Unfortunately, a greater number have published and advocated worthless systems.

More recently, Lawrence Revere's *Playing Blackjack as a Business* attempted to tie the state of the art together, with good results. This is also worthwhile reading.

As you peruse the strategy that follows, undoubtedly many plays will seem odd or illogical. It is vital to realize that the strategies presented are mathematically true, and must be followed. To deviate invites disaster. For an excellent treatment of theory in greater detail, consult Professor Thorp's book or Mr. Revere's. It is essential that you follow the strategy as shown.

4 Single Deck vs. Multiple Deck

Today in Las Vegas you can find blackjack games ranging from one to six decks. There are no single deck games in the Bahamas. The larger deck games are usually dealt from a shoe, and are far more common. One reason the casinos prefer multiple deck games is that reshuffling is less frequent, and therefore more hands are played per hour.

It is the author's preference to play single deck blackjack, although there are advantages to multiple deck play. Let's list the major differences:

1. Single deck blackjack avoids the necessity of converting the running count to a true count. This will be explained in a later chapter, but basically this refers to the fact that the relevance of a particular count total in multiple deck play is influenced by the number of half-decks remaining. To illustrate, assume the player is going head to head with the dealer; no one else is at the table. Four decks are shuffled and play begins. The player receives two small cards and the dealer's up card is also small.

The running count is therefore +3, as you will learn, but it can be seen that this advantage is considerably less meaningful than if the count was +3 towards the end of the shoe. (The end of the shoe is the last card in it and not the plastic card used to cut the decks. Depending on the number of decks in play, this may be up to a deck and a half.) To allow for this, the running count must be converted to a true count in multiple deck play.

2. It is easier to find a "clean" or less crowded table playing multiple deck blackjack, simply because there are more of them.

3. You will be watched more closely on a single deck table.

4. If you lose count early, which will happen, multiple deck play will increase the gravity of your error because you will have to play longer until the next reshuffle.

5. If you miscount early - and this is the killer - you will be playing incorrectly for many more hands than in a single deck game.

6. Statistically, there will be less variation in multiple deck play and the cards will tend to run "truer." Because there are more cards, there are more events which tend to even out the game.

7. The unseen burn card will have a greater effect on a single deck play.

8. Usually the higher stake tables ($25 or $100 minimum bet) are single deck tables. This is one reason why single deck games are watched more closely. If your bankroll permits, these tables are less crowded to play on.

9. Single deck games are dealt down to the player. Many multiple deck games are dealt up.

The emphasis in this book is on single deck blackjack. I think it is easier to learn and the overriding advantage is that a lost count or miscount affects fewer hands, as stated above. It should be pointed out that an occasional random count error has little effect overall, but this is only mentioned to be mathematically accurate. Don't rely on it.

A professional blackjack player knows how to beat both games. It is a mistake to attempt to master both until the player is proficient in one. Your decision may be based upon geographic considerations, if you live near places which only play multiple deck. If you think you have mastered one game or the other and are not making mistakes, but you are not winning after enough trials, you have mastered nothing. The scorecard has to be your dollar results.

5 Basic Strategy

The term basic strategy in blackjack is used to describe a decision table which has no regard for count. Such a table appears in this chapter. This table guides the player towards his maximum play without regard to the cards which have been played in previous hands; it is thus a no count strategy. It does, however, take into consideration the cards being played in the particular hand.

Basic strategy will just about break the player even, depending upon the individual casino rules. Under the most favorable Las Vegas casino rules, the player will actually have about a tenth of a percent edge. Essentially, though, it is a break-even strategy. It can be used for two purposes:

1. As a permanent strategy for the casual player.

2. For the card counter, when the count is lost, until the next shuffle.

The table only considers the player's two cards and the dealer's up card.

We must introduce some concepts now to define what a player's hand is composed of in order to read the tables correctly.

1. Any hand containing an ace is never considered by its total value. That is, a player hand of ace-seven (shown as A-7) is not 8 or soft 18 but A-7. A-4 is not 5 or soft 15 but A-4. This will become automatic after a little practice and is necessary to learn the charts correctly. You already do this by thinking of ace-ten as blackjack, not 21.

2. Likewise, most pairs are just pairs. 2-2 is not 4 but 2-2. 7-7 is not 14 but 7-7. You get the idea. Pairs will be split under certain circumstances and you must begin to think that way.

3. 4-4, 5-5 and T-T (T is any ten value card) are not pairs because they are never split. T-T is twenty and always stands. 5-5 is always 10 and may be doubled, but never split. 4-4 is always 8 and may be doubled, but never split.

There are 33 possible hands as recognized by our decision table. We do not recognize 8-6 as differing from 9-5, for example, both are 14. Note the table begins with 5 as the player's total, because anything smaller is really A-A, A-2, 2-2, or A-3, none of which are 2, 3 or 4.

Again, remember that for the first entry, 5 through 7 does not include A-4, A-5, A-6 or 3-3. These appear farther down in the table.

Here then, without further fanfare, is the single deck basic strategy decision table:

SINGLE DECK BASIC STRATEGY

Player Cards	Strategy
5 thru 8 except 4-4 and 5-3	Always hit.
4-4 or 5-3	Double (if dealer shows) 5 or 6, otherwise hit.
9	Double 2 thru 6, otherwise hit.
10 (including 5-5)	Double 2 thru 9, otherwise hit.
11	Always double.
12	Stand 4 thru 6, otherwise hit.
13 thru 16	Stand 2 thru 6, otherwise hit.
17 thru 20 (including T-T)	Always stand.
A-A	Always split.
2-2	Split 3 thru 7, otherwise hit.
3-3	Split 4 thru 7, otherwise hit.
6-6	Split 2 thru 6, otherwise hit.
7-7	Split 2 thru 7, stand 10, otherwise hit.
8-8	Always split.
9-9	Stand 7, 10 or A, otherwise split.
A-2, A-3, A-4, or A-5	Double 4 thru 6, otherwise hit.
A-6	Double 2 thru 6, otherwise hit.
A-7	Double 3 thru 6, hit 9 or 10, otherwise stand.
A-8	Double 6, otherwise stand.
A-9	Always stand.

Never take insurance, even on your own blackjack.

Do not memorize this table if your goal is to count cards. You will see later that is an approximation, a compromise of necessity. It is profitable to note a few characteristics of the table, though.

One of the primary things we can see from the strategy is that when the dealer shows 7 or better, we must hit until we reach 17. There will be one exception you will learn later when we advance to the count strategy table, but overall probably 80% of the game of blackjack under any strategy is to hit to seventeen when the dealer shows 7 or better. It can be shown by mathematical analysis that we must draw or be beaten. Drawing to seventeen always improves our chances; the player must count on being beaten otherwise.

The worst cards for the dealer are 4 through 6. These are bust cards. The tables take advantage of this by doubling down when we have the chance, or standing to avoid busting ourselves when we have hard 12 or better in these situations.

If you played basic strategy for awhile, you would notice that hit cards can throw you from one point in the table to another. For instance, assume a player 12 against a dealer 3. The player hits and receives an ace. Now the player has 13 vs. a 3 should stand. Assume A-2 against a 3. The player hits and receives a 4. The player now has the equivalent of A-6, which calls for a double against the 3. Since the player cannot double at this point, the table should be interpreted as a hit. Follow this logic and you will cover all possibilities. This can get a little tricky during pair splitting, especially aces, and requires practice.

If we were learning a multiple deck basic strategy, we would find that we would never double with an 8 total. This is because the removal of 4-4 or 5-3 from play has little effect on the remaining decks and the odds do not tilt in favor of doubling. There are about a dozen changes of this nature we would make from single deck strategy.

6 The Count

We have touched briefly on card counting and why this is required to win. Now you must learn how to do it.

It should be explained that several card counting systems have been devised, and that many of them work. Some are more accurate than others and will allow the player to win at a faster rate. The best card counting system for you is one you can master with a minimal or zero error rate.

The early winning card count systems counted fives or tens only. The reason fives can be successfully counted is because this is the single most pivotal card in the deck.

Surprised? It is true. Most people would think the aces are the most vital cards. Remove all the aces and play, and the player will be at a modest disadvantage. Remove the fives instead, and the house will lose steadily to basic strategy. This has been demonstrated on computers and is beyond dispute.

Most count systems today are based upon the ratio of tens to non-tens in the remaining deck. That is the key point. Some are needlessly complex; a few are complex and very effective. The author believes the Revere Advanced Point Count System the most effective and deadly system available, but it is virtually impossible to learn and play well. If you have a degree in mathematics (as Mr. Revere did) and scored over 700 on your college boards in math, get it later. You will probably win even with level bets and will not be spotted as a counter. You had better plan on devoting a significant part of your life to the system, though.

Slightly less effective but only slightly less complex are Professor Thorp's advanced point count strategies.

What you will learn here, in the author's opinion, is a workable balance between effective strategy and undue complexity. Undue complexity means an unacceptable rate of error when playing. That is the point of this book.

We need to know the ratio of tens to non-tens left in the deck at any particular point in play. We can do this by constantly computing a ratio as we go of tens to non-tens, but this is too hard. Therefore we will accomplish the same thing by counting small cards as well.

Small cards are defined as 2 through 6. We will regard 7 through 9 as neutral, which is an approximation and a compromise, but acceptable. Tens and aces are large cards.

To know the ongoing ratio of tens and aces to small cards, all we have to do is assign an equal but opposite value to each group. Therefore, we will count each ace or ten as minus one when we see it. A ten is an actual ten or face card. If we then count small cards as plus one when they appear, we will always know if the deck is good or bad by the current count total. A plus count is good for the player. The reason tens and aces are counted as negative numbers is because when we see them they are gone from the deck. Remember, we are interested in what remains, not what has been played.

We should stop here for a moment and reflect again on why the player has the advantage when the deck is ten (and ace) rich.

1. Blackjack pays three to two to the player but not to the dealer. Odds of drawing a blackjack are enhanced when the deck has a plus count. While this is equally true for the dealer as well as the player, the payoff favors the player.

2. When the count is plus two or greater (single deck), insurance is a favorable bet.

3. This reason is the most important: the dealer's chances of busting are greater when the deck is positive. So would your chances be, if you mimicked the dealer and drew up to 17 in all cases, but you will not. If you did draw to 17 all the time, you would not even warm your seat because you hit first, and if you bust, the hand is history. It matters not a whit if the dealer busts too; your chips are already in his rack.

Some count systems differentiate between the various small cards and allow differing values for each, such as the five. The seven through nine is not always neutral either. The good advanced point count systems do this and lead to improved accuracy, but again, the primary aim of this book is to teach a system you can learn and win with. If, at some future time you decide to play full time and can manage it, stick with Revere or Professor Thorp. They had help from M.I.T. and IBM.

Blackjack cards show singly and in pairs only. You must get used to counting this way. If you are playing single deck, where all player cards are down, you will see your two cards and the dealer's up card first. You will count all cards as you see them. Let me say that again:

YOU WILL COUNT ALL CARDS AS YOU SEE THEM.

When the initial deal is completed, you will have a three card count: your hand and the dealer's up card. As each player hits or stands in turn, you will see additional cards one at a time, as hit cards are always up. Should a player split or double down, he will turn up his two initial cards and you will see these in tandem. Count them as they show. When a player busts, he will turn over (or throw anywhere) his initial cards and these are counted as well.

Something needs to be pointed out here before we complete our deal. Often a player who busts will throw his cards down in such a manner that the top card obscures the bottom one. The dealer is supposed to spread these so they can be seen before putting them in the discard pile, but many do not. If this happens once, ignore it. If it happens again, leave the table because you cannot count what you cannot see. It goes without saying that it would not be helpful to your cause to ask him to spread the cards, although I just said it.

Back to sequence: the players have now finished and the dealer will turn up his bottom card. Count it. If he hits, you will continue to count each card as drawn. When play ends, the dealer will turn up all the player's down cards around the table, collecting or paying off as warranted. This is where the cards appear in pairs and must be counted that way. Count them. Be alert for a dealer who turns over player cards without spreading them. You will often notice that a pair of cards cancels itself out, such as a ten and a six. Plus one and minus one are zero.

There is actually quite a bit of time during this phase to count, as the dealer is busy with the chips.

OK, let's try something. Shuffle a deck of cards (you have been waiting for this). Turn over a single card and count it. Take as long as you like. Continue to turn over cards one at a time and count. The deck contains twenty small cards (+1), twenty aces and tens (-1), and twelve neutral cards (0). It follows then that when you turn over the last card, the count must neutralize to zero if you have counted correctly. Putting it another way which is a bit more fun, you should know in what category the last card is before turning it over: ace-ten, two through six, or seven through nine. Do this several times through the deck.

Next, turn the cards over two at a time. See how often a hand cancels itself out. Again, the last pair of cards should null the count to zero.

Repeat these exercises until you are able to count correctly most of the time. By then, you should be able to purchase the next edition of this book (not really). Eventually, you will be required to count correctly over 96% of the time under far more demanding conditions, while playing and betting, but at this point let's advance to the next step.

Deal a few hands around the kitchen table, after clearing the dinner crumbs. Pretend there are two other players and deal them in. (You should never play with more than this.) Pick up your hand and begin a count. Since you have dealt the other players down, you will have seen only the three cards mentioned above, your two and the dealer's up card. Arbitrarily hit one or both of the other players, even though you are unaware of their first two cards. Finish the hand in the sequence explained earlier. Take your time. The only important thing here is to nail down the sequence of counting. When you have completed, you will have a count number. Gather up all the cards used and reexamine them slowly to verify your count.

Do the above several times. Do not concern yourself with the time it takes. This is a concern of course later, but meaningless now.

Continue to practice this while you progress through the next chapters. After awhile, play only two hands: yours and the dealer's. You will have picked up the count sequence quickly with four players and it is more important to increase your playing speed with just two hands.

Later on you will see that the ability to see other player's down cards ahead of time is a useful weapon in your arsenal. You will find this can be done often. The only problem is that it tends to confuse what cards have been counted and what cards have not when the hand ends and the dealer turns up the down cards, since usually you will count all cards as they are upturned except your own. The best way to become adept at keeping the count straight in those situations is to play with other people, either at home or at low-stake tables in the casino.

Later, we will mesh everything together when we learn how to practice effectively. You will find counting is not hard to do right most of the time but hard to do right all of the time. Distractions are few at home but many and insidious at the casino. Do not be discouraged; counting accurately is the most demanding part of the game. Blackjack is not easy or everyone would win.

When you are getting the count right you will have taken the first step towards becoming what the casinos fear most: a card counter who is accurate.

7 The Plus-Minus Strategy

The single deck plus-minus strategy is the focal point of this book. It is an accurate winning strategy utilizing the plus-minus count we have learned (or at least looked at).

This strategy as depicted by the chart following must be memorized exactly. There is no substitute for this. You must learn it in its entirety as well as you know your own address or phone number. Even if you learn one line per night, you would still need only about a month to memorize it completely.

When you actually play, you will have many distractions and other things to think about such as betting and counting. The strategy table must be second nature and require no thought whatever. If you are confident in your knowledge of the plus-minus strategy, you will be less apt to miscount. Miscounting occurs when your mind is elsewhere. If you have to think about strategy, you will lose the count. Then you have less than nothing; you will lose. Ideally, keeping the correct count is all you want to have to concentrate on. You absolutely positively cannot do it unless you memorize the plus-minus strategy.

The chart itself dictates alternate courses of action in each given card situation depending on whether the count is positive or not.

At least one system is being taught in California which has four decision columns instead of the two we will use. The deck is classified as very rich, rich, poor or very poor. I met a graduate of this $500 course in Las Vegas. We ate breakfast together, and he told me he had been losing steadily for three weeks. He was going home that day. The interesting thing was that he still felt his system was the best available.

Maybe it was, but it did him no good. It seemed more complex than could practically be used without error. We were chatting about this at 7:10 AM next to the MGM Grand when the holocaust erupted there.

LEARN THIS CHART PERFECTLY.

SINGLE DECK PLUS-MINUS STRATEGY

Player Cards	Zero or Negative Count	Plus Count
5,6,7 or 6-2	Always hit.	Always hit.
5-3 or 4-4	Always hit.	Double (if dealer shows) 5 or 6, otherwise hit.
9	Double 5 or 6, otherwise hit.	Double 2 thru 6, otherwise hit.
10	Double 2 thru 7, otherwise hit.	Double 2 thru 9, otherwise hit.
11	Hit 10 or A, otherwise double.	Always double.
12	Always hit.	Stand 3 thru 6, otherwise hit.
13	Stand 5 or 6, otherwise hit.	Stand 2 thru 6, otherwise hit.

Player Cards	Zero or Negative Count	Plus Count
14	Stand 3 thru 6, otherwise hit.	Stand 2 thru 6, otherwise hit.
15	Stand 2 thru 6, otherwise hit.	Stand 2 thru 6, otherwise hit.
16	Stand 2 thru 6, otherwise hit.	Stand 2 thru 6, 10, otherwise hit.
A-A	Always split.	Always split.
2-2	Split 5 thru 7, otherwise hit.	Split 3 thru 7, otherwise hit.
3-3	Split 4 thru 7, otherwise hit.	Split 4 thru 7, otherwise hit.
6-6	Split 5 or 6, otherwise hit.	Split 2 thru 6, otherwise hit.
7-7	Split 2 thru 7, otherwise hit.	Split 2 thru 7, stand 10, otherwise hit.
8-8	Always split.	Always split.
9-9	Stand 2, 3, 7, 10, A, otherwise split.	Stand 7, 10, A, otherwise split.
A-2	Double 6, otherwise hit.	Double 4 thru 6, otherwise hit.
A-3	Double 5 or 6, otherwise hit.	Double 4 thru 6, otherwise hit.
A-4	Double 5 or 6, otherwise hit.	Double 3 thru 6, otherwise hit.
A-5	Double 5 or 6, otherwise hit.	Double 4 thru 6, otherwise hit.
A-6	Double 3 thru 6, otherwise hit.	Double 2 thru 6, otherwise hit.
A-7	Double 4 thru 6, hit 9, 10, A, otherwise stand.	Double 2 thru 6, hit 9 or 10, otherwise stand.
A-8	Always stand.	Double 4 thru 6, otherwise stand.
A-9	Always stand.	Always stand.

Take insurance if the count is +2 or greater.

There are certain keys that are helpful in memorizing this strategy. Note that all plays ending in the digit 6 (player's total) likewise end on the digit 6 in the strategy columns. Most split strategies end on a 7. All ace combination doubles end on 6. The plus column widens the range of action, never narrows it. A-3 through A-5 strategies are identical except for the A-4 plus column, where the 4 does not appear. Isn't that curious. You will find others, no doubt.

Later on when you actually use the chart you will find you will be hesitating for a moment before acting, even if you can recite the chart perfectly. The way our minds work, we tend to memorize in sequence and the stimulus for visualizing the strategy has not been the cards themselves. As you practice, the actual hands themselves will begin to condition your response and you will not have to visualize the table in order to act correctly.

This is an important point and emphasizes the need to practice your knowledge of the chart from actual card situations. We will go over this in detail in the Practice Techniques chapter.

If you compare the plus-minus strategy carefully with the basic strategy, you will see why the basic strategy is really a compromise. You must then decide what course of action you will take if you lose the count in play. If you feel that memorization of the basic strategy chart along with the plus-minus data would be too confusing, don't. Remember that the left hand strategy column for the plus-minus is for a zero or negative count. Zero can be considered no count with an acceptable accuracy loss. Play the left hand column when the count is lost until the deck is reshuffled. *Never* guess at the count.

If you feel you can safely memorize both strategies without confusing them, revert to the basic strategy when you lose count. The recommendation would be that you do not memorize the basic strategy if you are going to count. It is another source of error.

One final point. Some hands will appear much more often than others, as more combinations of cards comprise them. A 12 through 16 total in the player's hand is much more common than A-2 through A-6 or 2-2 through 6-6. While you must learn the entire chart perfectly, 8 through 16 must be learned double 100% perfectly.

8 Multiple Deck Modifications

You may decide that you would rather play multiple deck blackjack for a variety of reasons. I live on Florida's southeast coast, and the casino at Freeport is only 60 miles away. There are no single deck games there, and this certainly would be a more convenient location.

If you decide counting cards is not for you, and wish to learn basic strategy so that you will at least be in a position to hold your own at the tables, multiple deck basic strategy is presented here. You will still have about an even game, and will have a greater choice of tables to play on.

Also shown is the plus-minus strategy for multiple decks. To be precise, both strategies are for four decks.

FOUR DECK BASIC STRATEGY

Player Cards	Strategy
5 thru 8	Always hit.
9	Double (if dealer shows) 3 thru 6, otherwise hit.
10	Double 2 thru 9, otherwise hit.
11	Double all cards but ace. Hit against ace.
12	Stand 4 thru 6, otherwise hit.
13 thru 16	Stand 2 thru 6, otherwise hit.
17 thru 20 (including T-T)	Always stand.
A-A	Always split.
2-2	Split 4 thru 7, otherwise hit.
3-3	Split 4 thru 7, otherwise hit.
6-6	Split 3 thru 6, otherwise hit.
7-7	Split 2 thru 7, otherwise hit.
8-8	Always split.
9-9	Stand 7, 10 or A, otherwise split.
A-2, A-3	Double 5 or 6, otherwise hit.
A-4, A-5	Double 4 thru 6, otherwise hit.
A-6	Double 3 thru 6, otherwise hit.
A-7	Double 3 thru 6, hit 9, 10 or A, otherwise stand.
A-8	Always stand.
A-9	Always stand.

Never take insurance, even on your own blackjack.

Note some of the differences between the four deck basic strategy and the single deck version. See how the composition of the player 8 hand is not a factor in multiple deck blackjack? The removal of the 5-3 or 4-4 from the multiple deck does not affect things enough to warrant doubling down.

Do not use single deck basic strategy in a multiple deck game, or vice versa. There are enough changes between the two tables to make this unsuitable, and you will lose.

Following is the multiple deck plus-minus strategy table.

FOUR DECK PLUS-MINUS STRATEGY

Player Cards	Zero or Negative Count	Plus Count
5 thru 8	Always hit.	Always hit.
9	Double 5 or 6, otherwise hit.	Double 2 thru 6, otherwise hit.
10	Double 2 thru 8, otherwise hit.	Double 2 thru 9, otherwise hit.
11	Hit 10 or A, otherwise double.	Always double.
12	Always hit.	Stand 3 thru 6, otherwise hit.
13	Stand 5 or 6, otherwise hit.	Stand 2 thru 6, otherwise hit.
14	Stand 3 thru 6, otherwise hit.	Stand 2 thru 6, otherwise hit.
15	Stand 2 thru 6, otherwise hit.	Stand 2 thru 6, otherwise hit.
16	Stand 2 thru 6, otherwise hit.	Stand 2 thru 6, 10, otherwise hit.
A-A	Always split.	Always split.
2-2	Split 5 thru 7, otherwise hit.	Split 4 thru 7, otherwise hit.

Player Cards	Zero or Negative Count	Plus Count
3-3	Split 4 thru 7, otherwise hit.	Split 4 thru 7, otherwise hit.
6-6	Split 4 thru 6, otherwise hit.	Split 3 thru 6, otherwise hit.
7-7	Split 2 thru 7, otherwise hit.	Split 2 thru 7, otherwise hit.
8-8	Always split.	Always split.
9-9	Stand 2, 3, 7, 10 or A, otherwise split.	Stand 7, 10 or A, otherwise split.
A-2, A-3	Double 5 or 6, otherwise hit.	Double 5 or 6, otherwise hit.
A-4, A-5	Double 4 thru 6, otherwise hit.	Double 4 thru 6, otherwise hit.
A-6	Double 3 thru 6, otherwise hit.	Double 2 thru 6, otherwise hit.
A-7	Double 4 thru 6, hit 9, 10 or A, otherwise stand.	Double 2 thru 6, hit 9 or 10, otherwise stand.
A-8	Always stand.	Double 5 or 6, otherwise stand.
A-9	Always stand.	Always stand.

Take insurance if the true count is +1 or greater.

The same caution as stated earlier holds true for basic strategy. Do not use the multiple deck plus-minus strategy in a single deck game and vice versa.

The preceding table mentions the true count. When playing in a single deck game, it is not mandatory to adjust for the number of cards remaining when computing the count. As explained earlier, the significance of the count in a multiple deck game depends much more heavily on how many decks are being played with and, more importantly, how many decks remain. A count of +2 after the first hand of a four deck game is not nearly as advantageous as the same count total with only two hands left before the shuffle.

43

You must adjust for this. Converting the running count to the true count is done by dividing the running count by the estimated number of half-decks remaining in the shoe. If you are playing a four deck game, and one deck is estimated to have been used, divide the running count by 6, the number of half-decks remaining. The number should include the cards behind the plastic divider card.

This sounds harder than it really is. It is the only real extra complication you will have to worry about, as compared to single deck. Stack some decks together and soon you will be able to gauge the shoe.

As I have stated earlier, I prefer single deck blackjack. The primary reason is because of lost count situations. You may prefer the multiple deck game; it does have its advantages.

9 Betting

This chapter is concerned with the following points:

1. In a random chance situation, such as coin-flipping or break-even basic blackjack strategy, there is no betting system which will influence the long-range outcome.

2. When the player has a known advantage concerning the make-up of the remaining deck, he must bet more than when he does not or he will not win money.

3. The betting unit size should take into account the player's overall stake size.

4. Betting tactics are a major tip-off to the casinos as to who is counting cards and therefore strategy 2 above must be disguised.

We need to examine these points.

Many betting systems have been used and sold in an attempt to overcome the neutral or unfavorable odds that may exist with games of chance. None work. One of the most common tactics is known as the Small Martingale, which, by naming it, is overdignifying this tactic. It works like this: if you win, keep your winnings and leave your bet size alone. If you lose, double your bet until you win.

This would work but for one thing: all blackjack tables and all blackjack players (at least in the Western world) have a limit. Assume you are a $5 bettor and the table limit is $1,000. Assume also you have exactly $1,000. Lose nine straight hands - and you will, eventually - and you are egg salad. Win nine straight hands and you have won $45. Enough said?

Another system says do exactly the opposite and double up when you win, revert to your unit bet size when you lose. This is great. It guarantees you cannot win. The casinos will vie for the chance to fly you out and put you up if you want to do this and have enough money. Plan on staying one night, though.

Other betting systems of this nature are more subtle and on the surface appear to have some merit. A few are complex and involve visualizing things like different "banks." They are all less than worthless. Ask any high school math teacher.

If you are playing basic strategy, you may as well level bet because you will not know when the deck is in your favor. When deciding on your betting unit amount, it would be best to divide your total stake by perhaps 100 to avoid being cleaned out too fast when the cards run poorly. If you do win, you might then redivide your stake by 100 and increase your betting unit. Remember, none of this will change the odds of the game one iota. If you are really a sport, put the whole stake on one hand and walk away, win or lose. If you are in Las Vegas, spend the rest of the time enjoying the shows and visit the Hoover Dam. You should visit the Hoover Dam anyway.

Getting down to business, let us address the situation from the card counter's point of view. The counter knows when the odds have tilted in his favor and bets more accordingly. This will influence the eventual outcome and must be done. It is as essential as counting or playing the plus-minus strategy. These are the three components of the winning game.

The card counter must have patience and staying power. Patience is learned. Staying power is acquired by sensibly dividing up the overall stake so that an effective balance is achieved between underutilization of capital and over-extension and undue risk. If we research Revere and Thorp, we will find that both attempt to achieve this balance in slightly different ways. Revere recommends dividing the initial bankroll by 120 to arrive at the basic betting unit size, and playing no more than 30 units at any one session. The basic betting unit is always played until the deck becomes +2 or greater. Thorp varies this somewhat. Both recommend an orderly increase in bet size as the deck becomes and remains favorable, which is essential.

In the author's opinion, the betting progression for favorable deck play is partially dependent upon the particular playing conditions. This is so because the player does not want to be spotted as a potential card counter and not for any mathematical reason. If you are playing on a $2 table and the attention of the pit boss is elsewhere, and the dealer is yawning through the game, it is not necessary to be as cagy as when you are playing big money at high limit tables. This calls for a word about the "eye in the sky."

As you probably know, the glass over the tables in one-way and you may be starring in a video tape production every time you play. At least, count on the fact you are being taped. However, the tape is not constantly monitored but rather saved for replay should anything warrant a second look. When you read the chapter about casino deportment you will begin to see what to watch for.

This author recommends the following betting strategy in most situations:

Divide your initial stake by a number in the range of 100 and 120, depending upon the chip size this is closest to and your playing experience. Chips come in $1, $5, $25, and $100 denominations. For example, a $1000 stake into 100 pieces is a $10 unit bet. $1000 into 120 pieces is an $8.33 bet, which is unworkable. When beginning to play as a card counter, tend to be conservative and round down. $1500 should be played in $10 units, not $15, at first. Let your unit size grow with your experience and confidence. When you are comfortable at the tables with your strategy and have won, allow $1500 bankroll to play at $15. Do not go any higher than this, however. As you win, redivide your swollen bankroll again to come up with a new betting unit.

Never take more than one quarter of your stake to the table at any one time, which will be about 25-30 playing units. Never allow your basic unit bet to exceed 1% of the current bankroll. This should be done no matter how experienced you become. The odds do not favor the player that much and there will be times when a playing session results in a total loss. You are achieving the best balance in the manner described.

The betting progression is all-important. Again, a balance must be achieved between sensible escalation and seeking maximum advantage, tempered by the need to disguise what you are doing. To do this, we must take advantage of the fact that most players often naturally double their bet sizes when they win, by leaving the chips just won on the table for the next bet. Likewise, it is common for a player to double his bet size when he has lost in order to recoup.

Never increase your bet above the basic playing unit when the count is zero or negative. If thc deck becomes +1 when it is time to bet the next hand, increase your bct size to one and a half times the unit bet only if three conditions exist:

1. Chip denominations permit. If your basic unit is $10,

go to $15. If it is $5, leave it alone. A $25 player might go to $35.

2. There are no other players at the table.

3. At least two hands have already been played from the deck. (Single deck only.)

Never exceed one and a half times the unit bet with a +1 count; favorability of the deck does not warrant it especially at the beginning of a new deck.

If the deck becomes +2 or greater at betting time, you need to advance to a two unit bet. If you are coming off a win or a loss, this is a natural play. The only time you will not do this is when you are coming off a push, or tie. Never alter your bet size after a push, unless you are at a reshuffle. If you are under scrutiny, they will guess the reason why.

If you win the two unit bet, leave the chips for a four unit bet as long as the count remains +2 or greater. Never increase beyond four units. If you lose and the count remains at +2 or better, bet the four units again until the deck drops below +2 or is reshuffled. When shuffling occurs, revert to your basic unit bet. You may vary this somewhat if the count drops to +1 by going back to your 1.5 unit wager if you have played this way.

I have done something several times which I do not recommend, but you should have the benefit of this experience so you can make your own decision. When the count has gone appreciably negative, I have halved my unit bet when I felt this was safe.

You will note we have never jumped our bet more than twice the previous bet. We only bet four units when the count is +2 or greater and we have previously bet two units. We have never exceeded four units. We do not wish to jump from a one unit bet to a four unit bet under any circumstances, because this is a tip-off that you are a card counter. Remember, the count number increases in importance as the size of the remaining deck decreases.

10 Practice Techniques

Unless you follow this chapter and do what it says, this book will be nothing more than mildly interesting reading or worse, cost you money at the tables. The three components of successful blackjack must be melded together here and to do this requires performing two distinct exercises. One is primarily for counting and betting and the other is to nail down the plus-minus strategy table. You should begin by practicing the plus-minus strategy.

The last thing we want to do is actually use cards, for two reasons. They take an inordinate amount of time and the tough hands show only infrequently. Also, you must grade yourself and if you make an error you may not realize it. The answer is to use the test table of sample hands which appears here.

TEST TABLE

Problem No.	Your Hand	Dealer Shows	Your Action if 0 or Negative Count	Your Action If Plus Count
1.	14	3		
2.	2-2	8		
3.	6-3	5		
4.	A-5	5		
5.	9-9	5		
6.	8-3	T		
7.	13	3		
8.	16	5		
9.	2-2	3		
10.	7-7	5		
11.	A-7	5		
12.	14	A		
13.	9-2	6		
14.	9-9	A		
15.	8-8	T		
16.	4-4	2		
17.	14	4		
18.	A-9	6		
19.	7-3	8		
20.	5-5	7		
21.	16	4		
22.	3-3	5		
23.	A-8	2		
24.	6-6	5		
25.	12	6		
26.	A-A	2		
27.	6-2	6		

Problem No.	Your Hand	Dealer Shows	Your Action if 0 or Negative Count	Your Action If Plus Count
28.	4-4	6		
29.	A-6	6		
30.	A-4	4		
31.	2-2	4		
32.	6-3	4		
33.	5-4	8		
34.	A-2	5		
35.	6-6	2		
36.	15	9		
37.	9-9	3		
38.	9-2	8		
39.	A-6	3		
40.	12	5		
41.	14	2		
42.	A-A	9		
43.	15	8		
44.	3-3	7		
45.	2-2	5		
46.	A-5	6		
47.	9-9	6		
48.	16	T		
49.	7-4	5		
50.	5-3	3		
51.	6-5	7		
52.	7-7	3		
53.	2-2	6		
54.	A-7	2		
55.	13	6		
56.	A-A	7		

Problem No.	Your Hand	Dealer Shows	Your Action if 0 or Negative Count	Your Action If Plus Count
57.	5-3	5		
58.	A-4	5		
59.	A-7	3		
60.	2-2	7		
61.	16	9		
62.	9-9	2		
63.	A-5	3		
64.	7-4	2		
65.	14	9		
66.	7-2	3		
67.	A-7	6		
68.	2-2	2		
69.	6-4	5		
70.	7-7	6		
71.	9-9	7		
72.	A-4	6		
73.	7-7	2		
74.	16	7		
75.	A-2	3		
76.	15	A		
77.	15	T		
78.	A-8	6		
79.	6-6	4		
80.	7-2	7		
81.	A-4	2		
82.	3-3	3		
83.	15	3		
84.	14	8		
85.	4-4	5		

Problem No.	Your Hand	Dealer Shows	Your Action if 0 or Negative Count	Your Action If Plus Count
86.	6-2	5		
87.	A-A	A		
88.	5-3	6		
89.	7-3	3		
90.	10	9		
91.	3-3	4		
92.	7-7	4		
93.	A-7	4		
94.	15	6		
95.	A-3	6		
96.	13	8		
97.	12	4		
98.	A-6	4		
99.	14	T		
100.	8-3	3		
101.	14	6		
102.	7-7	8		
103.	A-7	T		
104.	5-5	2		
105.	A-8	3		
106.	4-4	3		
107.	15	2		
108.	7-3	A		
109.	A-8	4		
110.	16	8		
111.	A-5	4		
112.	7-2	6		
113.	3-3	6		
114.	A-6	5		

Problem No.	Your Hand	Dealer Shows	Your Action if 0 or Negative Count	Your Action If Plus Count
115.	8-3	9		
116.	4-4	7		
117.	13	2		
118.	15	4		
119.	8-2	6		
120.	12	3		
121.	14	7		
122.	9-9	4		
123.	A-7	A		
124.	13	A		
125.	3-3	8		
126.	13	5		
127.	15	5		
128.	A-6	2		
129.	6-5	4		
130.	13	4		
131.	A-A	3		
132.	3-3	2		
133.	5-4	2		
134.	8-2	4		
135.	16	6		
136.	A-3	4		
137.	16	3		
138.	A-8	5		
139.	16	A		
140.	7-4	A		
141.	15	7		
142.	4-4	4		
143.	12	2		

Problem No.	Your Hand	Dealer Shows	Your Action if 0 or Negative Count	Your Action If Plus Count
144.	A-A	T		
145.	5-3	4		
146.	A-4	3		
147.	14	5		
148.	6-3	T		
149.	A-2	4		
150.	16	2		
151.	A-2	6		
152.	6-6	6		
153.	A-3	5		
154.	6-6	7		
155.	A-3	3		
156.	6-6	3		

The preceding table depicts a full variety of blackjack situations. No reference is given to count. You must go through the table in any order and write down the correct response, whether hit, stand, double or split. If you are practicing basic strategy, there will be a single set of answers. If you are learning and practicing the plus-minus strategy, you will have a dual set of answers depending on if you assume the count is positive or not. The correct answers for the plus-minus strategy are shown in the appendix. Basic strategy players, who have taken the easy way out, are penalized by having to determine the right answers themselves.

When you think you have memorized the plus-minus strategy (or basic strategy), begin to go through the chart. You will doubtless make many errors. You will begin to see that your response must be triggered by the cards themselves rather than the order in which you memorized the strategy chart. You will say, "Oh, darn, I knew that!" many times, or something similar. All this is expected. Take your time. At first you should have no regard for the clock. After awhile, begin to log the time it takes to complete the test against the number of errors you make. Progress will be slow. Expect it. Accuracy must outweigh speed. Speed can never be at the expense of accuracy. As in anything else, speed will come naturally. While the faster you can complete the test error-free (if ever) is an indication of how well you know the material, keep in mind that during actual game conditions you will have plenty of time. People hem and haw all the time and in fact this helps disguise your actions.

Alter the sequence in which you go through the table. Try it while watching TV. Vary the conditions - you will not be able to play under constant ideal conditions all the time.

It would be a reasonable estimate that you will have to test yourself perhaps 25 times before you even begin to feel comfortable that you know the strategy. And this is after you have the chart memorized. When you can answer all the problems correctly (that's right - no errors) rapidly twice in a row you will be ready.

If you realize that probably 99% of all would-be counters never get this far, you will have a powerful incentive.

The second exercise to perform is to actually play blackjack against yourself. You will do this to pin down two things: the count and the bet. You will need a rack of chips, a table, a deck of cards and an understanding family. Use a single deck even if you plan on playing multiple deck blackjack. Play through to the end of the deck for one reason only, which is to verify your count. Remember the count should revert to zero with the 52nd card. Pay yourself off when you win and pay the house when you lose. Begin play with 30 units. Bet as instructed. The end result will not be true because in actual play the deck will be shuffled before the end; at home you will be able to take maximum advantage of favorable decks. Play to the end, however, to verify the count. Most of the hands at the end of the deck will be incomplete so treat those bets as void.

By doing this you will be combining all elements of the game. I recommend playing in two half hour sessions per night until you are proficient. Concurrently you should be practicing with the table in this chapter.

Before you go on a gambling trip, practice with a deck of cards for one week. While you should reach a point with the test table where you have mastered the strategy, practicing the count is ongoing.

If you can do the above proficiently you are what you set out to be. You will be able to beat the game of blackjack.

11 Casino Deportment and Other Odds & Ends

The last time you saw the word deportment was probably on your sixth grade report card. It graded your behavior.

In a very real sense, your deportment in the casino will have an effect on your success. In the most extreme case, you can be barred and will not be able to play again. Then you are out of business. I have never been barred, but have come close. How you behave, how you observe the things that go on about you, how you choose a table to play, what you drink; these can help make the difference between winning and losing.

I have tried to learn something new each time I have played. I will pass along to you some things which should enhance your chances of success.

I do not like to play in the Bahamas and I do not play in New Jersey. Perhaps this is an unfair judgment of Atlantic City because I have never gambled there. But I do read the papers and talk to people. The Wall St. Journal has reported wholesale barring of suspected card counters. In Atlantic City, the cards cannot be shuffled early as a defense against counters by regulation. The casinos seem to have overreacted by barring players on suspicion. I am also told the tables are overcrowded.

The Bahamas have some unfavorable rules, such as restricting doubling down to certain situations, but this can be compensated for. The biggest problem is overcrowding. Unlike Las Vegas, the casinos close late at night when traffic is thin. The card counter needs an uncrowded table, as you have learned. If you are playing in the "third base" seat (the seventh and last) and you have placed your bet when the deck was +2 with a full table, by the time you get your first card the deck can conceivably be -4. In the Bahamas the crowds seem to come in waves as the various cruise ships disgorge. To my mind, it is an acceptable place to practice for low stakes only. It will expose you to difficult conditions.

The casino in Port-au-Prince is a bit untidy and if you look closely on the dealer's shirt you may see a spot of lunch. I have only played there once, and have no opinion as to playing conditions overall.

I have played in London. It is a magic city but the tables are jammed beyond belief, even on weekday nights. The English are used to queueing up, and I suppose they are used to losing at blackjack.

Therefore the rest of this chapter concerns itself with Las Vegas.

It is almost impossible to get the proper amount of sleep in Las Vegas. Adrenalin begins to flow as the airplane banks over the city, and the strip hotels looming up towards the sky come into view. Like a betraying woman, they seem to beckon and grasp for your wallet, while promising allure and adventure. The city is devoted to gambling and other forms of pleasure, and never closes. It hardly slows down. You can play at any hour of the day or night, and probably will.

The slot machine music begins in the airline terminal. The taxicab takes you past more neon than exists in whole countries. You must pass through the casino to get anywhere in your hotel. By the time you get situated and unpacked in your room, the urge to lunge out and play is almost irresistible. The casinos are well aware of this and here is where their first bit of psychological strategy is usually employed. No matter when you arrive, your room will in all likelihood not be ready and your luggage will go into a hold area for perhaps several hours. You will be standing around the front desk about ten feet from the first slot machine with no place to go. You have just completed a long plane ride, waited around with your luggage for a taxi, ridden to the hotel, and waited in line to check in. About the only place to go is in the casino, and all your money is burning a hole in your pocket. Your mental state is about equivalent to an iguana, especially if you have changed time zones.

This is when they want you.

Don't go in the casino.

When you finally get to your room, take a shower and stretch out for awhile, or sit out by the pool soaking up the sun. When you feel ready, mentally review the decision table and deal yourself a deck in your room to refresh the count sequence.

When you begin, play small. Be a $2 bettor or less until you gain your rhythm and confidence.

If you live on the east coast, it is a mistake to think you can stick to your own time zone so that you arise early enough to find uncrowded playing conditions. You may awaken on Eastern time, but you will go to bed on Pacific time. There are no clocks in the casinos, and no one even notices.

Let's get into some specifics, beginning with your choice of table. Before you sit down, you must know how many decks are being played with. Most multiple decks are dealt from a shoe, but this is not the case with a two-deck game. Two decks are held in the dealer's hand, and can look like one deck. If you are in doubt, ask. If you approach a table where no one is playing, the cards will be spread out on the table in a fan. If two decks are being used, you may see two fans, but don't assume this to always be true. Again, don't be hesitant to ask.

The next decision is where to sit. It is customary advice to the card counter to sit at third base, so he has the advantage of seeing more cards when it is his turn to play. The problem here is twofold: the casinos know this and sometimes it is difficult to see all the way across the table. Also, this assumes player cards are being dealt up.

I personally sit in the middle. If I am alone at the table, the empty seats on either side are not quite as inviting as if I were on the end and the entire table to my right is empty. A head-to-head game is ideal, and the counter wants to prolong this condition as long as possible. People are funny and tend to congregate. Many times almost all open tables will be crowded but a few are empty. If the player sits down, beginning a game at a virgin table, it seems only a few moments before the seats begin to fill.

There is an advantage when you sit in the middle at a single deck table. As you know, the player cards are always dealt down here. If you sit in the middle and there are two other players, one on either side, much of the time you will be able to read their hands when they pick them up. This is not possible at third base. You enhance your chances of being able to do this if you smile or engage in brief conversation with the other players. You must be a student of human nature. You will have established a brief comradeship with them; after all you are all playing against the house. They will not tend to hug their cards to their breast. By seeing the cards of those around you, you have enhanced your odds.

Notice one thing before you sit down. There is a great variance between dealers as to the speed at which they work. The slower the better, at least at first. If the game is in progress, note how fast the dealer operates and make sure you can keep up. If you cannot, move on. Women especially can deal nice and slowly, especially if someone is talking to them. One on one play can be extremely rapid, and you may be uncomfortable in this setting at first.

Now you are there and finally ready to play. Buy in at a shuffle with the 25% or so of your stake. Watch the shuffle and notice how the faces of the cards are never lifted from the plane of the table, so that you cannot see any of them. The dealer will now burn a card, and this is where one of the significant advantages of playing single deck blackjack comes into play.

In multiple deck blackjack, the burn card is removed and placed in the discard pile at the dealer's right. In some single deck games, this is also true. But in other games the burn card is inverted and turned over to the bottom of the deck. This is the only point at which any card violates being parallel to the plane of the table, and many times you can see it. If you can read this card, you have gained an advantage. You have a count before play begins. This can only be done with a minority of dealers and if you find one stick with him, if other playing conditions permit.

Now you are finally playing. You need to know about some things during play.

This is one of them. During one of the first times I ever played serious blackjack, I noticed something. The dealer had a ten value card showing and in this situation he must check for blackjack. When he does this, he is required to lift only the corner of his down card while shielding it with his other hand, which is holding the deck. The dealer did so, and then did it again slowly. When he eventually turned up his down card at the conclusion of the hand, it was a 4.

I didn't get it. It happened again the next day. When I got back to my room I placed a four face down and picked up the corner to see what the dealer saw, which by now you have probably realized. The top of a four looks much like the top of an ace, and the dealer had to check twice.

Since that time, I have kept track of what the down card has been when the dealer has had to take a second look. In about 80% of the cases, it has been the four. Once it was a five. On another occasion, the dealer actually had a blackjack which she did not call at the time. She called over the pit boss and explained what had happened. She said she thought the down card was a four. The pit boss, whose function it is to arbitrate such unusual events, ruled that she had to play the hand as 21 instead of blackjack. No one at the table had doubled down or split a pair, thereby putting twice as much money at risk, so there was no argument.

In my opinion, it is appropriate to assume the dealer has a bust hand when this occurs. Proceed accordingly by treating the dealer's hand as if the up card is a four, not ten. Hit, stand, double or split as required by the decision table. I know of no other source which advocates this, and you may wish to disregard it. I suggest seeing for yourself.

How long should you play at any one session? It depends. If you lose the 30 or so playing units, definitely quit. You may be making mistakes and not realizing it. The body is an unreliable indicator of fatigue here because you are in a stress situation. You may feel alert but you are not. At home, you would yawn and attention would wander. At the tables, adrenalin brings about a false feeling of alertness.

If you are winning, you have another problem to worry about - being spotted as a counter. No one much cares what you do if you lose, unless you are flagrant in your actions. Begin to win, though, especially on the green or black chip tables, and eyes turn upon you. This is one reason why it is not advisable to play too long at one table (or casino) if you are winning. A good rule of thumb would be to quit when you have doubled your 30 units. If you are breaking even or nearly so, bag the session after about an hour unless you continue for practice only. As stated before, be alert for fatigue, which sounds like a contradiction. The first indication is losing the count, which means you are having difficulty concentrating. If you make a strategy error, stop. You need to rest and review.

I once made two strategy errors during the same session, back when I first began card counting and did not have the sense to know when to stop. I remember them well and they cost me money.

I had been playing in a poorly lit casino with $750 for about an hour, which was about 20 minutes too long. I felt alert, and was maintaining the count properly. The deck finally became favorable and my bet size progressed to $100. I was dealt a ten and a three. The dealer showed a three. My mind went blank. Not only was I tired but the four green chips on the line made me nervous.

It seemed that millions of decision rules ran through my mind all at once, but none concerned the 13. The count, which had been +2 at the beginning of the hand, was currently zero as the player to my right had a blackjack and I had seen the player's hand to my left. I knew I was on the left side of the decision table.

After about a hundred years, I finally stood, vaguely thinking of the 14 rule. The dealer turned up a ten and hit, drawing a 7 for a total of 20. I just about popped a filling grinding my teeth when the 13 rule flashed cruelly through my mind: I should have stood on a 5 or 6 only and the dunderhead error had made a $200 difference in my bankroll.

The $200 was an expensive lesson but not enough of one, it seemed. I made another strategy error a few minutes later and finally had the sense to stop. Pretend this happened to you and let my loss be your gain.

You may read or hear that the doubling strategies on A-2 through A-5 are a bit dangerous and may tip you off as a potential counter. That is because they are somewhat unusual plays and are not intuitive to the uninformed player. It is my opinion that this is no longer true. Doubling on A-2 through A-5 is a common occurrence nowadays. However, I did run into potential trouble twice with A-7 and A-8.

People who deal blackjack treat their job like people who do anything else. Dealing is their source of income and they seldom do anything to jeopardize it. Many are cordial and seem to root for you, groaning when they pull a blackjack or four card 21. However, they are trained to spot certain actions and many will report them.

During the course of play one afternoon I had a A-7 vs. the dealer's 2. The count was positive. I turned over my cards to double. The dealer called out to the pit boss "Soft 18 hit here" and waited. The pit boss came over and watched. I lost the hand, and mumbled something about the fact that I must be tired to have doubled on 18. The pit boss nodded imperceptibly and moved away.

That is the funny thing about those guys. If you pull an unusual play and lose, even though correct, they will not worry about it. It is as though you have been proven an idiot. If you win, though, they will continue to watch.

A lot of this is psychological. We tend to notice what we can see and forget what we cannot. The eye in the sky is seeing all but we become concerned with the pit boss. Even if the pit boss walks away from something like I have just described, the tape may be monitored. Be aware of this. A pit boss may move away for just that reason.

Allow me to give you an example of just how clever the casinos can be. One morning I sat down to play in a casino whose hotel I was staying at. Because I was staying there, I tended to play more there than elsewhere, a mistake I have learned to correct. The dealer looked familiar. He said hello as he shuffled, and said he hoped he dealt me better cards than the garbage he had dealt me two nights ago. I had no memory of this. He told me that I played very well considering all the fives I drew. Again, I told him I did not remember this and expressed surprise that he did. I was then told I purchased $300 in chips, played for 42 minutes, and cashed out at $325. I leaned back and stared at him for a moment, and finally said, "Are you trying to tell me something?"

"Maybe," was the reply with the look a parent gives his child when he is caught chewing gum with his braces on, or whatever. Then I recalled that we had had a pleasant conversation during the game about football, since this particular dealer used to play professionally. He was passing me a kindly warning that my winnings were being tracked.

Needless to say, I played no more at that establishment for the duration of the trip.

The casinos work in three shifts. Do not rely on this fact and treat a different shift as playing in a different casino. That is because the shifts are staggered, usually by one hour, between the dealers and the pit bosses. That is ample time to pass along any information about you.

You will also find that when you leave a table the dealer always offers to change your chips, ostensibly so that you don't have to lug around a big stack of $5's or $25's. Sometimes they will say this, and it appears to be a thoughtful courtesy. It is usually not. You are cashed out for one reason only: to find out how much you have won or lost. If you have lost, go ahead and do it. If you are significantly ahead, try to avoid this. You can say "No thanks, I'm just going to another table" or the men's room or something. If you have begun play by pulling chips out of your pocket, you can put some back during play and this will help muddy the situation. If you are with your wife you can give her some presumably to go play on another table. You get the idea. Like anything else in life, though, don't overdo it. If you do cash in at the table, don't appear concerned. Just don't argue.

It is usually recommended that you tip the dealer. This is considered good form when you are winning, although I have never seen a dealer tip a player who is losing. It is a better idea to bet for the dealer, so he rides with you. You do this by putting the dealer wager just outside the betting area towards the dealer, before the insurance arc. Doing this cannot hurt and may help. There is one thing you should be aware of, though.

Dealers do not keep their tips individually except when they are on overtime, as a rule. Tips and bet winnings go into a common pool, so the individual dealer is just not that concerned with the small change. If you are a $25 bettor and are regularly betting $5 for the dealer, this will be appreciated. The dealer has only so much latitude as to how far down into the deck he can deal, but the $5 bets may help. Forget this with an occasional $1.

If you can catch a dealer on overtime you have a different situation. The ideal is an overtime head-to-head game. If you want to know if the dealer is working late, just ask him. He will be glad to tell you and knows what you mean. He is likely not *that* loyal to his employer.

If you think about what happened in Atlantic City during 1980 you will realize how important dealing down as far as possible really is. Early shuffles ruin your game and may be warning you are under scrutiny. So is a new dealer at an irregular time. Leave.

I don't want to name individual casinos here, for conditions change all the time who knows when you are reading this, but certain casinos have their own characteristics on the Las Vegas strip. As of this writing, single deck blackjack is found in about a half dozen casinos on the strip and many places downtown. You can get the flavor of a casino rather quickly. A large number of $2 tables or less will mean that heavy money is likely to be noticed more, especially at slack times. This is another mistake I have made. I put down $1,000 for an afternoon weekday session and it was as if I walked in naked, or my money was covered with visible germs. The casino was catering to the $2 bettor. Two pit bosses stood by. They looked at me as though they were staring at a wanted poster and expected the fugitive to come in the door shortly. I did not play long. And this was on the strip.

In other places $1,000 is no big deal. As I have said, look over the denominations of the various tables and you will get a feel for this.

If your stake is not large you will find weekend play is difficult and crowded. You may catch a barren table but this is not likely. If you play at odd hours, such as 5 AM or so, this is helpful but remember that fewer personnel will be working and the sparse number of open tables may be busy. With a larger stake you have better playing conditions, because fewer people can afford to play at the higher minimum tables. This means a lot and can make the difference between winning and losing. On my last trip to the strip I managed an uninterrupted two hours at a solitary single deck table, because the minimum was $100. It was about 10 AM and I was fresh and alert. The smaller stake tables were filled.

A caution here. If you do arise early and begin play at 5 AM, it is best to appear as though you have been up all night. I don't want to overdramatize the situation, but a freshly shaved and dapper appearance at that time is not the norm. The obvious conclusion is that you have arisen early to play blackjack alone and they may wonder why.

Some casinos are poorly lit, or have poorly lit sections. Try to avoid these if you can. Even if you think you can see all the cards, you may miss a few and in any event poor lighting increases the strain you will be under. There is one casino just off the strip which is lit about as well as a night club. Treat it as such.

If you play enough and reflect on the overall picture, you will realize that psychology is a crafty and powerful tool used by the casinos. The goal is to get you comfortably to the tables and then make you uncomfortable in small ways. If you are a moderate drinker, the girl will ply you with alcohol regularly. If you are not and merely want coffee or water, you will wait almost forever. Cigarettes are usually available because smoking dulls the senses and distracts you with matches, ashtrays, and ashes. There is never a good place to put an ash tray, and the smoke always blows in someone's face. As a pilot, I can tell you that oxygen is recommended for smoking pilots at altitudes as much as 2,000 feet below non-smokers.

The pit boss serves several functions. A few are designed to comfort the heavy money players while they lose. Human nature again. Because a pit boss calls a customer by name, he may stay longer and lose another wad before leaving. But he has been made to feel important, identifying with the house. The pit boss also intimidates. We have discussed this. I watched a player once who was being obviously observed by the pit boss. Finally, the player called him over and asked the boss what he was doing. The man was taken aback, and finally said something inoffensive. The player turned to me and said loudly, "These guys all think they are in a James Cagney movie." The pit boss turned on his heel and walked away. He did not bother our table again.

You may feel intimidated if you think you have something to hide. I was asked by one pit boss why I doubled on a soft nineteen. I replied that I had read somewhere that this should be done. This satisfied him. Only counters are feared.

Once, when I think I was suspected as a counter, an attempt was made to intimidate me. I bought into a game for $500. The dealer spread my money on the table and called "$500 green out," as they will. The pit boss strolled over, looked at the money for awhile, and whispered in the dealer's ear while cupping his hand over his mouth. Very unusual. Then he stayed around watching the game for about ten minutes. I got the message and cashed out shortly after he walked away. I waited that long to let him know that he was not intimidating me, which was not smart. Pride bested sense. When I did cash out, I exchanged some reds ($5) and greens ($25) for black. The girl called out again and the pit boss came over and observed the transaction. They wanted me to know they were logging my chips. What they didn't know was that there were 8 greens in my pocket.

If you play for awhile, you will realize the single most important indicator of how alert you are is the frequency with which you lose count. A tough hand involving pair-splitting and perhaps secondary splitting can cause you to lose count while you are concentrating on the strategy, unless you are totally facile in this knowledge. If you are beginning to lose the count, quit. You are tired. This rule must not be violated, and it is the single most common reason for losing. If you know the strategy perfectly and bet as prescribed, miscounting is the only thing that will beat you in the long run.

It goes without saying that drinking alcoholic beverages while playing serious blackjack is to be avoided. If you want to drink and have any chance of winning while gambling, shoot craps, bet the don't pass line, and give the odds. You will almost have an even bet and this takes no concentration.

If you live far from Las Vegas, so that transportation is a significant expense, you may wish to consider a junket. On a junket, the casino may pick up your tab for transportation, lodging, food, drinks and shows. This is a good deal only if you do not count cards. A basic strategy player may find a junket attractive. Amounts vary, but at the present writing between $5,000 and $10,000 will suffice to qualify you.

Some junkets have elaborate rules. I was reading one recently which required a minimum of three hours play per day, with an average bet of $50 per hand. The junket allows the casino to keep close tabs on your gaming success. Each time you sit down to play you are supposed to ask for a marker, so that chips left over from previous play are not used. This makes it easy for the casino. You can see how the card counter must not avail himself of this otherwise attractive set-up.

When you play, try to relax. The more you can consider the chips as just chips and not money, or its equivalent in goods, the better you will play. There is an ebb and flow to the tide of blackjack, as seems to be the case with other gambling games. Subjectively, it will appear that nine out of ten decks are negative even though this is not really the case. If you play well, it will seem as though you are holding your own for long periods of time punctuated by a few very favorable situations, which will jump your playing bankroll to the next plateau. If you bet correctly and have the appreciable amount of patience required, you will be able to take advantage of these situations. It will be frustrating to play for a stretch with all the skill you have and not be winning, especially when some drunk comes up and plunks down $500 on a single hand and wins. This usually happens just when a deck has turned favorable after a dry spell, and the other player walks up from nowhere and takes the good cards. Naturally, he walks away and leaves you with garbage. Be comforted in the knowledge that probability says he will leave more than he has won somewhere else.

I hope the material in this chapter is of some value to you. As you gain from experience, many impressions will be formed in your own mind. I have tried to give you some of mine.

12 Playing With a Partner

The idea of playing with a partner can be appealing from the point of view of lending confidence to the fledgling player. It is always tougher to go almost anything new alone, and no doubt a partner can lend moral support to the solitary challenge against the house. However, using a partner should be regarded as a counter-measure rather than an initial strategy of attack. This is because playing in tandem carries disadvantages and has only one principal benefit: avoidance of detection.

If two players working in collusion play at the same table, both are placed at a disadvantage. This is for the same reason that the effective blackjack player seeks a solitary table with no other players. Each partner dilutes or potentially dilutes favorable count situations, as we have previously discussed. The betting unit size is of no consequence since a single player can simply bet twice as much as a duo, except when the bet is limited by the table maximum.

It can be argued that two players can cash in on very favorable decks when the count is extremely positive.

However, the majority of the time the deck fluctuates around the neutral count mark and so the very favorable situations occur only infrequently. Use of a partner in these limited situations may be acceptable but it should be noted that the deck is likely to be shuffled earlier by the dealer simply because more cards are required per complete hand with the addition of each player; a single player can more effectively play one on one in these occurrences, in any event. Also, dealers have a tendency to shuffle when a new player enters the game if the deck is not new. We can safely say that mathematically there is no advantage to partnership play unless the table maximum is limiting the bet, and in fact the players are disadvantaged in partnership play because of dilution.

Nonetheless, human beings being what they are, you may decide you wish to play with a partner at some stage, whether to gain moral support or to assist each other through the learning process. If so, it is essential to play with an individual whose knowledge of the strategy is as perfect as yours - and if you are playing for money your knowledge is perfect, is it not? You both must be playing the identical system so that your relative bet sizes coincide and you can check each other in this manner from hand to hand. It is also paramount to sit so that you can each see the other's cards and increase you knowledge of the count, if playing single deck where the cards are down. After each session, notes can be compared on particularly relevant hands and this may help cut down any errors you may be making, especially at first, whether in the count or the decision table strategy.

It should be realized that two players whose progressive bet sizes are coincident will enhance the chance of detection.

The really legitimate use of a partner occurs when you are a steady winner and suspect you are being observed. If you become a successful master of the game, this will occur sooner or later. When this does happen, use a partner as a counterstrategy in the following manner.

Only one player sits at a particular table and bets modestly. When the count becomes appreciably positive, the player gives a signal to his compatriot who is stationed nearby observing, ostensibly, some other game. At that point the second player enters the game with a large wager, and continues to bet heavily until the original player signals the count has dipped below +2. Then the partner leaves. No suspicion will fall onto the heavy bettor, since he had no opportunity to count the cards from previous hands. Likewise, he will not have gone from modest bet sizes to large wagers but rather jumped into the game cold. You can see this strategy can be quite effective, at least for a short time, at each casino. It cannot be used forever, though, as eventually the link-up will be made by casino personnel.

The particular signal used can be left to your imagination; scratching the head, etc. Just make sure your partner does not have dandruff or habitually scratches; this can have dumbfounding results.

One of the key things to remember about partnership play is that it will not work as well in single deck games as on multiple deck tables. This is due to the tendency of the dealer to reshuffle at will in single deck play and the fewer number of cards available for play. Often the deck will be shuffled as new players enter the game.

There is a sophisticated variation using a partner which can be deadly if circumstances are right. It is difficult to master and I will not describe it in detail because it is unlikely you will use it until you have really become an expert blackjack player.

The broad outline of this variation revolves about the use of a partner at the same table whose basic betting unit size is much smaller than that of the key player.

The "dummy" partner is in the game strictly to use up the cards in negative count situations and to sit out when the deck becomes positive. This player must be an absolutely perfect counter and also somewhat of an actor. You may have noticed I have not emphasized "types" of players in this book, but in this situation the dummy player must fit certain requirements to avoid detection. The principal one is the this player is a woman.

Women have made excellent blackjack players: their concentration can be fierce and they seem to have a natural aptitude for the repetitive nature of the game. They are also better actors than men, as most men can say from experience. However, we are concerned with perception here rather than reality. A chatty female will be classified by most pit bosses as a nowhere player and stands a much better chance of working effectively by betting small amounts and passing up hands from time to time. The effect of this strategy is almost as good as if the principal player bet and withdrew at will on a particular table, avoiding negative count situations and betting plus hands only. The dummy partner also takes up a seat and can discourage other patrons from entering the game. There are certain strategy rules which would apply here, similar to the strategy tables we have studied.

An ultimate in sophisticated blackjack partnership play involves the use of three team members: the dummy, the principal player, and the partner not at the table who awaits the signal to swoop into the game while the dummy either passes out, goes to the ladies room, or powders her whatever, All of this requires sophistication, much practice and error-free play.

The recommendation in this book is that you play alone for quite awhile until you have built confidence and your bankroll. You must be self-assured in your play as a completely independent functional unit for all facets of the game. Emotional factors must not be an influence and the use of a partner should be dictated by strategy alone.

I have seldom engaged in partnership play; one reason is that I am not personally acquainted with very many proficient player I would risk my money with. The better one becomes the less inclined he is to talk about it; there is no fraternity of good players. When I have played with a partner the results were good but in the end I could have done as well alone. Your case may be different.

13 Cheating and Mechanical Aids

In the past few years, I have made acquaintance with with several blackjack dealers at the major league Las Vegas casinos. During our many conversations, the subject of casino cheating has arisen. From these and my own experience, I can categorically state that if cheating is ever performed in the strip casinos, the average line dealer is unaware of it.

Many authors have claimed they were dealt seconds or otherwise taken advantage of. I believe this is untrue and the players were mistaken. I cannot speak for all areas of the world, of course, but on the Las Vegas strip it should be assumed that all games are honest.

The casinos have much to lose by cheating. The gaming license is of course the paramount item. Also, word travels fast and a rumor of cheating can have an effect on business. In low stakes games, the risk is not worth the reward. In the big games, the players may have enough status to make large waves if they are cheated.

No doubt, the hand is quicker than the eye as any of us can attest who have watched the card magicians. However, the ear can be an aid to detection when the suspicion is that seconds are being dealt. In a quiet casino, the sound of the cards can be heard as they are dealt in a single deck game and the sound of a second cannot be disguised. Try this yourself and you will know what to listen for. Of course, this possibility only exists with hand-held decks and not a multiple deck shoe game.

If you are off the strip and are concerned about this subject, watch for an irregular dealer change. While dealer changes are staggered, the time at the table is fairly constant for each dealer. In order to cheat, the casino has to substitute a crooked dealer. Then listen for seconds or watch for a disappearing deck. At no time following the shuffle is the deck supposed to disappear from view. If this happens, the deal is irregular and you should either ask for a reshuffle or leave.

The sum and substance of the above is that you are not going to be cheated on the Las Vegas strip. If the casino does not want you, it will bar you.

Regarding mechanical aids, several clever devices have been used to assist the player in maintaining a proper count. These range from sophisticated electronic gear to simple clues such as the position of a pack of cigarettes or arrangement of chips. One player I know quite well owns a simple watch calculator purchased over the counter and worn on the wrist. I have watched him use this. He actually adds and subtracts from the count with no attempt to disguise. He has never been accosted and continues to do this to the present day. To me, this is amazing and is asking for trouble. Yet he seems to get away with it.

I strongly recommend that no mechanical aids be used to assist in maintaining the count. A properly trained player needs no assistance and finds any device a distraction.

As a pilot, I have found over the years that the level of sophistication of cockpit instrumentation has increased dramatically. This is all well and good, but there is a price to pay. Failure of the support devices carries an increasing penalty as related to safety. The pilot, to a large extent, has become a systems manager in a mobile office. The basic skills of the profession can erode and leave one in a disadvantaged position with equipment failure.

This is less dramatic but equally true for the serious blackjack player. You have no business wagering big money if you need mechanical assistance. Referring to outside indicators adds distraction and ultimately confusion, and you can count on this occurring at the worst possible time. You do not need it.

Psychologically, the almost unavoidable result of using a count-assist device is fear. Tangible evidence of card-counting leads to fear of detection and can result in a losing game. The successful card counter should be serene and self-confident that all factors of a winning game are developed mental talents which cannot be detected or lost.

Memorization of the strategy tables can be readily accomplished and the self-tests shown previously will lead to a comprehensive working knowledge of this facet of the game. The rules for betting are straightforward and readily understood. That is why the count alone is frequently augmented by outside aids; it is the only part of the game which must be computed on an ongoing basis during play. The exercise of playing against yourself described earlier is essential practice as proof of maintaining the count. If you have practiced properly and the last card nulls the count to zero with regularity, you will be able to maintain the count. It can be confusing at first when playing in the casino with other players despite your previous practice; the setting is different and it may seem as though cards are everywhere - appearing and disappearing with disconcerting speed. That is why it must be emphasized you should begin play for small stakes.

Even a properly prepared player can be discouraged initially under actual game conditions, and it should be expected that the count will be difficult to follow. Do not be overly concerned; a few sessions totalling perhaps two hours will overcome this difficulty. If you are playing for small stakes it is well worth the price. You will be able to move with confidence to the higher minimum games once the count sequence is established in the real arena.

There are many players who can win at home but not in the casino. Invariably the problem is failure to maintain the correct count. Persistence is the key; these players have given up too easily and many resort to some sort of counting aid. In a low stakes game you will become relaxed fairly quickly and find your own rhythm at count maintenance. You will not have to worry about your bankroll and can concentrate on the count. You will already have learned and practiced 95% of this skill; allow yourself to polish your talents for relatively little money - you may win anyway as you learn.

When I travel to Las Vegas, I still do this for perhaps a full day before indulging in any serious gambling. I ignore the rule not to play with more than two other players. A full table gives one an excellent opportunity to practice under rapid and difficult conditions. I have kept no track of these low stakes practice games but would venture a guess that even these have resulted in no overall loss. If you do this before moving to the serious phase, you will have gained the most important intangible aid to a winning game: confidence.

Once again, do not attempt to count cards by using any outside indicators. You can do it eventually by yourself. Once you have, you will win.

When you stagger over to the cashier's cage with a full load of chips you will know what I mean by confidence.

14 Who is The Grey Knight and Why Should We Believe Him?

The Grey Knight rides alone and at night. I can still play blackjack and have never been barred in any casino. If I used my real name this would end.

I do not play blackjack for a living, and became intrigued by blackjack quite by accident. I play when I can. I make no excessive claims as to my success, but I can say that of this writing I have never completed a gambling trip without making a profit, since I began card counting. My average gain has been about 55%. This does not include prior jaunts, when, like (probably) you, I won and lost with no coherent system and only luck to assist me.

This book began as a syllabus for a blackjack course I was teaching. It seemed to grow by itself. It is my first book, and I doubt that J.D. Salinger is going to call me for any writing tips. Creating great American literature was not the aim of this work, but rather the presentation of a clear learning path guided my thoughts.

You should believe the material because it is accurate. If you have doubts about card counting, research the newspapers concerning the Atlantic City debacle. This should convince you that card counting works and that the material can be learned and applied effectively. The casinos make enough profit and I hope some of it winds up in your pocket as well as mine.

15 Conclusion

Blackjack is a serious business and a big business. To play well, you should treat it as such because the casinos do. If you follow this book, you will have invested many hours of practice and achieved a level of skill that should be compensated for. If you are barred, you will have lost your investment.

This happened to a friend of mine. He had won only $1500 when he became yesterday's lunch. He can only play overseas now, which puts front money at risk for travel.

The goal of this book has been, as stated many times, to teach you to play winning blackjack , with emphasis on the single deck game. The book might have been a lot thicker by presenting miscellaneous anecdotes or delving further into theory. This can be gleaned elsewhere, notably from Professor Thorp or Mr. Revere's work. You do not need any other material.

I hope I have done my job by clearly showing you yours. Do it, and the rewards will more than justify the effort.

16 Appendix

ANSWERS TO TEST TABLE
Single Deck Plus-Minus

Problem No.	Your Action if 0 or Negative Count	Your Action if Plus Count	Basic Strategy
1.	Stand	Stand	
2.	Hit	Hit	
3.	Double	Double	
4.	Double	Double	
5.	Split	Split	
6.	Hit	Double	
7.	Hit	Stand	
8.	Stand	Stand	
9.	Hit	Split	
10.	Split	Split	
11.	Double	Double	
12.	Hit	Hit	

Problem No.	Your Action if 0 or Negative Count	Your Action if Plus Count	Basic Strateg
13.	Double	Double	
14.	Stand	Stand	
15.	Split	Split	
16.	Hit	Hit	
17.	Stand	Stand	
18.	Stand	Stand	
19.	Hit	Double	
20.	Double	Double	
21.	Stand	Stand	
22.	Split	Split	
23.	Stand	Stand	
24.	Split	Split	
25.	Hit	Stand	
26.	Split	Split	
27.	Hit	Hit	
28.	Hit	Double	
29.	Double	Double	
30.	Hit	Double	
31.	Hit	Split	
32.	Hit	Double	
33.	Hit	Hit	
34.	Hit	Double	
35.	Hit	Split	
36.	Hit	Hit	
37.	Stand	Split	
38.	Double	Double	
39.	Double	Double	
40.	Hit	Stand	
41.	Hit	Stand	

Problem No.	Your Action if 0 or Negative Count	Your Action if Plus Count	Basic Strategy
42.	Split	Split	
43.	Hit	Hit	
44.	Split	Split	
45.	Split	Split	
46.	Double	Double	
47.	Split	Split	
48.	Hit	Stand	
49.	Double	Double	
50.	Hit	Hit	
51.	Double	Double	
52.	Split	Split	
53.	Split	Split	
54.	Stand	Double	
55.	Stand	Stand	
56.	Split	Split	
57.	Hit	Double	
58.	Double	Double	
59.	Stand	Double	
60.	Split	Split	
61.	Hit	Hit	
62.	Stand	Split	
63.	Hit	Hit	
64.	Double	Double	
65.	Hit	Hit	
66.	Hit	Double	
67.	Double	Double	
68.	Hit	Hit	
69.	Double	Double	
70.	Split	Split	

Problem No.	Your Action if 0 or Negative Count	Your Action if Plus Count	Basic Strategy
71.	Stand	Stand	
72.	Double	Double	
73.	Split	Split	
74.	Hit	Hit	
75.	Hit	Hit	
76.	Hit	Hit	
77.	Hit	Hit	
78.	Stand	Double	
79.	Hit	Split	
80.	Hit	Hit	
81.	Hit	Hit	
82.	Hit	Hit	
83.	Stand	Stand	
84.	Hit	Hit	
85.	Hit	Double	
86.	Hit	Hit	
87.	Split	Split	
88.	Hit	Double	
89.	Double	Double	
90.	Hit	Double	
91.	Split	Split	
92.	Split	Split	
93.	Double	Double	
94.	Stand	Stand	
95.	Double	Double	
96.	Hit	Hit	
97.	Hit	Stand	
98.	Double	Double	
99.	Hit	Hit	

Problem No.	Your Action if 0 or Negative Count	Your Action if Plus Count	Basic Strategy
100.	Double	Double	
101.	Stand	Stand	
102.	Hit	Hit	
103.	Hit	Hit	
104.	Double	Double	
105.	Stand	Stand	
106.	Hit	Hit	
107.	Stand	Stand	
108.	Hit	Hit	
109.	Stand	Double	
110.	Hit	Hit	
111.	Hit	Double	
112.	Double	Double	
113.	Split	Split	
114.	Double	Double	
115.	Double	Double	
116.	Hit	Hit	
117.	Hit	Stand	
118.	Stand	Stand	
119.	Double	Double	
120.	Hit	Stand	
121.	Hit	Hit	
122.	Split	Split	
123.	Hit	Stand	
124.	Hit	Hit	
125.	Hit	Hit	
126.	Stand	Stand	
127.	Stand	Stand	
128.	Hit	Double	

Problem No.	Your Action if 0 or Negative Count	Your Action if Plus Count	Basic Strategy
129.	Double	Double	
130.	Hit	Stand	
131.	Split	Split	
132.	Hit	Hit	
133.	Hit	Double	
134.	Double	Double	
135.	Stand	Stand	
136.	Hit	Double	
137.	Stand	Stand	
138.	Stand	Double	
139.	Hit	Hit	
140.	Hit	Double	
141.	Hit	Hit	
142.	Hit	Hit	
143.	Hit	Hit	
144.	Split	Split	
145.	Hit	Hit	
146.	Hit	Double	
147.	Stand	Stand	
148.	Hit	Hit	
149.	Hit	Double	
150.	Stand	Stand	
151.	Double	Double	
152.	Split	Split	
153.	Double	Double	
154.	Hit	Hit	
155.	Hit	Hit	
156.	Hit	Split	